Ethereum Trade and Investment – The Ins and Outs

What You Need To Know

Introduction - What's Inside The Book

"Like most of you reading this book, I'm just a regular guy with a regular day job. I began my investing career, more of a hobby really when I got my first paycheck at age 15 and opened my first bank account. I've expanded my horizons as I've gone through life, especially with a wife, a mortgage, and kids.

I believe in "smart investing" – this means no get-rich-quick schemes but also not passively letting your money sit idle in a checking account or your grandmother's mattress. A smart investor studies before executing any potential trade and understands the risks and rewards that come with investing. I developed an interest in cryptocurrencies after learning of Bitcoin several years ago. I was fortunate enough to "get in" early in the game and sold many of my Bitcoins at a handsome profit, though I still hold a fair number as well.

My knowledge of Bitcoin lead me down the path of other cryptocurrencies before I came across the Ethereum platform. As I will explain in the book, Ethereum sets itself apart from other similar networks through its use of smart contracts. This is why I believe that Ether, the cryptocurrency that Ethereum requires to operate, is a smart investment to add to a well-diversified portfolio.

This book should NOT be construed as just plain investing advice. I am in no way advocating that you should throw your life savings in cryptocurrencies or raid the retirement fund for this purpose. You may even finish this book and decide that

Ether is not for you, and that's completely fine. This book is meant to be a guide and a starting point to enter the exciting world of cryptocurrency investing. It begins with a background on what cryptocurrencies are, then is followed with a description of Ethereum. I hope you find this book as useful as I found it fun to write!"

Copyright 2016 by Ben Abner All rights reserved.

This document is geared towards providing exact and reliable information in regards to the topic and issue covered. The publication is sold with the idea that the publisher is not required to render accounting, officially permitted, or otherwise, qualified services. If advice is necessary, legal or professional, a practiced individual in the profession should be ordered.

- From a Declaration of Principles which was accepted and approved equally by a Committee of the American Bar Association and a Committee of Publishers and Associations. In no way is it legal to reproduce, duplicate, or transmit any part of this document in either electronic means or in printed format. Recording of this publication is strictly prohibited and any storage of this document is not allowed unless with written permission from the publisher. All rights reserved.

The information provided herein is stated to be truthful and consistent, in that any liability, in terms of inattention or otherwise, by any usage or abuse of any policies, processes, or directions contained within is the solitary and utter responsibility of the recipient reader. Under no circumstances will any legal responsibility or blame be held against the publisher for any reparation, damages, or monetary loss due to the information herein, either directly or indirectly.

Respective authors own all copyrights not held by the publisher.
The information herein is offered for informational purposes solely, and is universal as so. The presentation of the information is without contract or any type of guarantee assurance. The trademarks that are used are without any consent, and the publication of the trademark is without permission or backing by the trademark owner. All trademarks and brands within this book are for clarifying purposes only and are the owned by the owners themselves, not affiliated with this document.

Contents

Introduction - What's Inside The Book ii

Chapter 1 - Understanding fully what Cryptocurrency Is 1

Chapter 2 - Ethereum Coin - What is it? 7

    History 7

    Applications 9

    Smart Investment 10

Chapter 3 - How To Get Ethereum Coins 12

    Mining 13

    Trading 14

    Investing 16

Chapter 4 - What You Need To Get Started 18

    Wallets 20

Chapter 5 - The Pros and Cons of Ethereum Trading 23

    Pro's 24

    Cons 25

Chapter 6 - Final Thoughts 28

Conclusion 30

Chapter 1 - Understanding fully what Cryptocurrency Is

Imagine this sort of scenario. You have several different kinds of money on hand that you could use to purchase goods and services with. The main one you probably deal with all the time. This is the sort of money that you use to purchase goods with all the time and is the sort that is still massively popular, even in the digital age. It's paper money, and metal coins, such as dollars, quarters, and the like. You simply hand over your exact change, and the person who you're purchasing from takes it tallies it, gives you back what you overspent.

The second sort of money that you might have on hand comes in the form of nonphysical forms, such as credit cards, debit cards, coupons, vouchers, or gift cards. These sort of forms of money are still physical, but the money on them is stored either somewhere else, or have a balanced digitally ingrained on them that you draw from when you use them for purchasing. In the form of Debit Cards and Credit cards, the money itself is stored based on your bank balances and what you have tied currently to that card. Whereas gift cards, vouchers, and the like have a set limit on them that you can purchase from with them. In some of these cases (such as debit and credit cards), you can use them again and again as long as the money is connected to them.

The third, and fastest growing form of currently is known as a cryptocurrency. Imagine that you have a way to pay entirely through digital means that cannot be traced back to you, leaving you not only anonymous, but also have something that acts like money and currently in the real physical world in that its monetary value fluctuates, making it more or less valuable on a daily basis, yet you can still use it to purchase goods and services with.

Of course, you might be asking yourself then: What is a cryptocurrency? What makes it special?

Both very valid questions to ask.

Cryptocurrency is typically defined as a digital currency that's derived from encryption techniques that have a set amount of generation "hashes" on them, meaning there can only be a certain amount in circulation at a time, but is still earned through entirely digital means. This means that every crypto coin (usually known as an "altcoin") is simply lines of code that have a monetary value attached to them, making them valuable for certain commodities.

Another way of understanding them is also to learn a little bit about their history as well.

Historically, cryptocurrency like objects have been around since the rise of the internet back in the late 90's, when the internet was quickly being developed as a tool that was used for more than just passing the time. In 1998, a proto-concept of cryptocurrency was developed by Wei Dai, a Chinese Developer, dubbed "B-money". It showed promise, but at the time there was no way to produce it in a safe way that couldn't be duplicated easily. Quickly after that, another developer named Nick Szabo created what he called "Bit Gold", which was like the bitcoin and other cryptocurrencies that would soon follow, mostly utilizing a "proof of work" function built into its coding that for the most part prevented the currency from easily being duplicated in mass quantities.

Shortly thereafter in 2009, a developed using the pseudonym Satoshi Nakamoto developed what would be known as "Bitcoin" using an SHA-256 cryptographic hash function, which was a natural progression from earlier systems used by Bit Gold, and B-Money, and made it virtually impossible to attempt to duplicate, using the proof of work function developed earlier.

Within 2 years of Bitcoins launch, and success on a global scale to be used as a decentralized currency. Other coins quickly followed using the same functions as Bitcoin itself. Namecoin, Litecoin, Peercoin, and others were soon derived from Bitcoin itself, even standing out from other coins in differences of how they functioned, as well as differences in use as well. In fact, eventually even "funny" or humorist approaches to the cryptocoin soon became popular on the cryptocoin scene. Coins such as "Dogecoin", "Pandacoin", or even "Trumpcoin" started to become well known, and traded. Even earning monetary value themselves in the process despite the inherently silly nature of their names and the cause of their creations.

However, what all cryptocurrencies since share in common are that they all on some level hold monetary value as they cannot be replicated, duplicated, or simply created out of thin air.

That then begs another question then: Is this all legal?

Yes, and no.

It actually depends on predominately where you are in the world and local laws.

See, the problem with Cryptocurrencies is because of how they're earned, traded, and even held onto, it exempts them from local taxes. If you held $100 in an investment, you could be taxed a percentage of your investment to the government. If you held onto 100 altcoins, and their value goes up, no one but you earn's that increase in value, and if you trade it or use it to purchase it, no one has to pay taxes on the transaction.

Because of this, many different countries around the world are still undecided on what exactly to classify cryptocurrencies and still have them be wholly undefined. This is made even more difficult to even approach due to the fact that cryptocurrencies are not dependent on the country's economic strength. An altcoin is worth the same throughout the world. This dependence on the internet and the exemption to taxation has even made the trading, distribution, or selling of cryptocurrencies illegal in some parts of the world, as a real fear of them destabilizing the economies of certain nations is seen as a very real threat. In fact, in Russia, it's illegal to purchase anything other than with the Russian ruble, and even holding cryptocurrencies can grant you jail time.

What makes it even more dangerous legally is also the fact that new cryptocurrencies are being developed all the time as well, which makes any sort of regulation next to impossible as a fear of oversaturation could potentially lead to an economic collapse. This is actually seen all the time in various different economic models, so it's a real possibility that governments have to keep a tight control on. This might not make sense, especially if it seems that investing in cryptocurrencies is producing something in return, but it's actually been seen very often. Let's use for example a product that's developed that will promise to revolutionize the way people do things in their homes. We'll assume this product does several things, and it's something that everyone believes that they need, so initially they start to buy the product and start to use it, leading to a lot of happy customers. This drives in investors, who see the potential for this product, so they bring in and invest in the business, hoping to earn more money in return. Some people believe they can take this product (Dubbed Product X), and improve on it and sell it on the market. So they re-engineer Product X, and introduce Product B. This begins a new cycle, as people either leave product X for Product B and adopt it, or it brings in new customers and investors for Product B. Suddenly, you have Product C on the market, followed with Product D, all the way to Product Q, and everyone has some version of the product, but no company has majority market share enough to justify the production of the product, and investor confidence disappears, eliminating capital for new businesses, and Product X and it's derivatives disappear from the market.

Another major problem also comes from the anonymous nature of cryptocurrencies, and the very real fear that it could be used for illegal purposes. In fact, it's even been reported by several major organizations that criminals would take their money, invest in cryptocurrencies, and then "sell it" to another person, often an accomplice, and effectively launder money in that manner. Not to mention because it's exchanged through digital means via the internet and holds real world monetary value off of the internet, criminals can also use various cryptocurrencies as a way to purchase illegal products such as drugs, weapons, and more. So it's only natural that most governments of the world want to have some way to regulate the market. This, of course, has been started to make some headway in the United States under the Securities and Exchange Commission, which in 2013 claimed that cryptocurrencies (mostly Bitcoin) were considered an alternative form of currency and could be liable for oversite, especially in the use of fraud or outright theft of the altcoins.

All in all, though, trading, earning, and even using Cryptocurrencies is perfectly legal in most parts of the western world. In this book we're actually going to take a look at one major cryptocurrency that's been seeing massive rise in trade since its inception that is a good investment for people to invest in:

Ethereum Coin

Chapter 2 - Ethereum Coin - What is it?

You might now be asking yourself about Ethereum coin, and what it is, and that's a very valid question. What makes it so different from all the other cryptocurrencies and altcoins that are out there on the market?

After all, with Bitcoin leading the pack as the first coin on the market, and a slew of other coins that you could invest in, what makes Ethereum special enough to stand out of the pack and be considered something special?

The answer to that is pretty simple. What makes Ethereum better is how it's utilized on a grand scale, and how it enables users to intuitively have control over their pool of Ethereum wealth that no other cryptocurrency can compete with.

History

To put it in perspective, let's take a little bit of a look back at its history and where it got its start.

Back in 2013 a programmed named Vitalik Buterin who was involved with the Bitcoin project when it first got off of the ground believed in a decentralized coin that could actually be continued to be expanded on. At the time, part of the problem Mr. Buterin was seeing with bitcoin was it was becoming mainstream, and accepted slowly as an alternative to conventional methods of holding wealth. While initially, this was the goal with Bitcoin, the fact that it could become completely centralized under a government control was part of the problem, he felt and severely limiting what Bitcoin was supposed to initially revolutionize.

So in March of 2014, Ethereum was being fully developed and was brought on board as a project that could have the potential to extend blockchain use (The main way that "miners" mine for bitcoin or other cryptocurrencies) beyond the traditional peer-to-peer limitation of the altcoin coding. While legal issues and questions arose to both its legality what Ethereum could possibly even do, it soon became apparent that it was a legitimate project after Buterin won the "World Technology Award" for the creation of Ethereum.

Soon after, crowdfunding for the project began to start pouring in in July to August of 2014, with initial investors pooling in their bitcoins to purchase in Ethereum coins. The end of the crowdfunding event happened on September 2nd, 2014 at the conclusion of nearly $20million in sales generated from just Bitcoin purchases alone,

By the end of May 2016, Ethereum market value quickly rose to more than 1 billion USD. It was quickly becoming a serious contender against Bitcoin itself, mostly due in part to the various different services that the Ethereum platform promises that Bitcoin itself cannot do. Today, it's still being developed on and maintained, but each new service that's created centralized around Ethereum continues to prove it's staying power over other competing Altcoins who can't keep up.

Applications

So now you have a bit of understanding of where it came from, what can it do? What applications are being talked about that make it worth investing time and money into?

As well as being a traditional cryptocurrency that you can hold on you like any other one on the market, the Ethereum platform has a wide range of different uses to them other than simply being a digital object that you can possess. In hypothetical uses, Ethereum is mostly used with higher end software that can be used to establish online marketing platforms, where instead of traditional uses where you open a store, tie it to your bank and tax information and social security and stuff, you simply open up a trading wallet, and trade Ethereum for goods and services quickly and efficiently.

In other uses, it's seen mostly in having a way to enjoy having access to a decentralized monetary system that's not tied to any government oversight. This allows Ethereum to be traded for a wide range of different objects, even physical ones. It's not unusual to see it quickly used for projects in finances in lieu of physical currency, identity management, electricity and resource allocation, gambling betting, and even used for arts, crafts, and even food. In fact, some musical artists like Imogen Heap and other independent artists used Ethereum trading for their music in lieu of traditional currencies.

Because it's easy to work with, easy to use, and easy to trade you can even use it to bypass business models that normally would be too costly to run as well. With Ethereum, you don't have to worry about import/export taxes, sales taxes, and you can even create smart applications and contracts that won't require a lawyer's fee as well to understand.

Smart Investment

So with all of those choices, applications, and information that was previously shown, how widespread is it? After all, it doesn't really do any good if anyone invests in it, but you still can't use it for anything other than the group of people who still have it. It's no more valuable than owning a handful of Carnival Tokens. They look pretty, but they have limited application.

True, while the New York Times noted in march of 2016 that the Ethereum platform adoption is still in its early phases and mentioned that its complexity might be too ambitious, the fact that various companies, institutions, and other organizations having faith in the Ethereum platform gives more credibility to the cryptocurrency over its other competitors, even over Bitcoin.

in fact, Microsoft announced a partnership with ConsensSys, a blockchain startup focused on the Ethereum technology, to help develop a cloud-based computer business model to allow people who use cryptocurrencies to trade their coins for Microsoft services, including securities, OS applications, cross-border payments, trading, and more. Even allowing a way for the technology to be used within the Microsoft Visual Studio programming packages as well.

Not only that, but ConsenSys is also using the Ethereum platform as well to help create by 2017 a fully functioning digital bank to be allowed to store, trade, and even invest in Ethereum and other cryptocurrencies as well.

While there are still a lot of initial problems to the platform itself, it's successes have outweighed heavily the negatives, and shows that investing in Ethereum is something that's considered a smart choice for the future.

Chapter 3 - How To Get Ethereum Coins

So now you've read in previous chapters what cryptocurrencies are, what Ethereum is, learned a bit of basic history about them both, as well as come to understand what it is they do exactly. Assuming that you're continuing to read this chapter and show interest in investing and trading in Ethereum, the next logical step would be to discover how to obtain Ethereum then

After all, it's not like any other form of investment or currency. You don't get a hold of it, and physically hold it in your hand to use whenever you want. It's also not an investment option that has any form of certification like stocks, bonds, or IRA's or 401(k)'s either. It's all held digitally, and that means that you own it on your computer.

Fair enough. But how do you even start to obtain them? It has to come from somewhere. Physical currencies are simply IOU's printed off from the government based on the strength of its economy. You can't print off or copy, or digitally get a hold of Ethereum coins through normal means.

Luckily, though, they're three major ways that you can get a hold of Ethereum coins. We'll be taking a quick look at each of their applications, how to earn them, and even a little bit of information about their pros and cons.

Mining

Technically, Mining isn't what you think it would be. It's not about grabbing heavy tools, and going out and digging in the earth for the valuable Ethereum coins and all. As has been mentioned before, Ethereum coins are an entirely digital thing that you can only get through the internet, and can only hold on your computer.

So then what exactly IS mining for coins exactly?

Mining is a technical term. In normal circumstances with physical currency, governments print more money and base it off the strength of their economy. With cryptocurrencies though mining is one of the main ways that they're able to make/discover more altcoins. Of course, like with traditional real life mining you will be competing with other miners to earn coins.

How does it work?

Simple. Whenever we send Ethereum coins to one another or do any sort of transaction with the coins, a little bit of information known as a hash gets left behind. Collecting enough of these hashes on the end of each transaction eventually gets collected by the Ethereum network and stores itself as a sort of "block", which miners then use to chip away at using mining applications from their computer to earn bitcoins a little bit at a time before eventually the entire block falls apart, the parts are distributed, and everyone gets their share that they put in.

However, keep in mind that the basics of that are a lot more complicated than simply finding the block and having access to it. That's more or less a simplified version of how the process goes, and mining is very CPU intensive. You essentially need networked computers put together, or at least a CPU that's built almost exclusively towards mining the Ethereum coins. Luckily, though, there's the possibility of joining a mining pool where everyone pools resources together and shares in earning coins together.

All in all, though, while Mining is very complicated (and deserves it's own e-book in its own right), it's also very slow and takes an initial investment just to get started. While you can literally start with nothing but a powerful PC and internet access, there are other ways to invest in Ethereum.

Trading

Trading is a very lucrative way of earning Ethereum coins. Simply put, you have a goods or service that someone wants, and they give you a payment for that. It's really that easy. It's just like traditional currency transactions.

The only downside to it is that Ethereum coins fluctuate in prices on a daily basis. One day you'll be earning more coins due to the fluctuation of the market, while the next day you'll earn considerably less than what you intended before the market goes on an upswing. This happens normally in real life daily too, as most currencies are in a state of fluctuation, but there are usually limits in place to keep it from being too drastic too quickly.

Let's put this into an example. Let's say you offer I.T work for professionals and help maintain networks. You charge 5 Ethereum Coins at the current market value of what they're worth. They go up in value, meaning that the Ethereum you earned before are worth more than they were a bit ago. At the same time though, while the Ethereum coin is worth more, your services are still judged based on outside influences, such as other real world currencies (Such as the U.S Dollar, or EU Euro) and so, your services are expected to remain the same price, thus lowering your prices from 5 Ethereum to a possible 3 Ethereum.

Technically, that's not bad. You're still earning the same as you were before, just less Ethereum coins. But, don't be so hasty to celebrate your good fortune, because soon the market swings against your favor and Ethereum coins drop below in price, well below what they initially started at when you offered your I.T services. Now the three that you earned from before are worth considerably less than before, meaning you're earning less for the same amount of work.

Of course, the upside of this is that you can again adjust your price to even higher than you had them at than initially, and the market might once again swing in your favor, making the coins you saved worth even more than before.

Which brings us to another way of getting Ethereum coins that are similar in the same vein, but entirely different.

Investing

Investing in Ethereum coins is pretty simple. You simply purchase them based on their current monetary value, trading them out for another currency, and then you hold onto it hoping the value of Ethereum coins rise's enough to have justified the purchase. That's it. That's all there really is when it comes to Ethereum investing.

Though, it does get a little bit deeper than that to be quite honest. It's more than just holding onto them and hoarding them. After all, if everyone just hoarded their Ethereum coins like some sort of digital dragon, then they wouldn't really rise in price after all. They'd just be expensively and needlessly complicated toys. With investing you have to at least be a part of the reason to stimulate the market. So generally it's acceptable to take your invested Ethereum coin, and even use it as part of the market itself.

However, at the same time, it's through investing such as this that drives the price of Ethereum coins up, and makes it more valuable as well as their use as an actual currency that draws people in. So don't be afraid to take what you've invested in, and even use some occasionally to stimulate the market for other goods and services, or even sell some off yourself to other interested parties should the value increase. The more people that are involved, and the more people are invested in the Ethereum platform, the more they'll be worth in the future.

Chapter 4 - What You Need To Get Started

So, if you're still up to this Chapter, that assumes that you're interested in Ethereum trading and investing into the cryptocurrency platform still. If that's the case, you might be asking yourself "Great. How do I get started?"

Getting started is the easy part, and out of everything in this guide, something you can do right now with nothing more than what you have and no extra cost.

The first thing you'll need to do to get started is to decide how you intend to earn Ethereum Coins. Do you want to perform Ethereum mining, using your computer and it's resources to compete with other miners for parts of a coin before being able to fully put it together? Do you want to just start offering services through the internet and sell your skills and products to earn them? Or do you have disposable income in more traditional currencies that you want to use to purchase them through the internet instead and simply hold onto them? Do you want to do a combination of both of them?

The answer really depends on your intentions, because each decision requires different resources.

With mining, it's all dependent on your computer and it's CPU power. Naturally, weaker and older computers will continually be lagging behind in terms of power and might not be able to mine efficiently enough to justify the cost and time you're putting into mining. The programs that you'll be tasked with running aren't just something you put in the background of your computer and go about your day. They require the full power of every available resource your computer has and will be running them at full capacity. To a lot of Ethereum coin miners, they generally buy one or two very powerful CPU's and use them both as dedicated mining machines, built for no other purposes. Sometimes they'll pool their collective resources together and join what's called a "pool" where other people link up their computers and perform mining tasks together, doling out coins equally among all other members. Other miners buy server space from other people and use the server itself as a tool for mining if they don't have the funds or time to dedicate to a mining computer rig. In a lot of ways, unless you have the computer already designed for mining and time and dedication to mining itself, the cost of mining can quickly outweigh what you'd get in return. Sometimes the effort isn't worth it, but that all does depend on other factors.

In every other case, all you really need is access to the internet and a decent computer on the low to midrange. Most of what else you need only takes up a certain amount of information and can be accessed much like any other internet application.

With that said, the next thing you need to focus on is what sort of wallet system you want to use.

Wallets

Now, what is a wallet? It's been mentioned before in this e-book, but not touched on too much. Is it like a traditional wallet that's used to store money in it?

Yes, and no.

Traditional wallets are generally just that. They hold your finances easily in one place, as well as other information. Digital wallets are used much in the same way but are heavily specialized in holding cryptocurrencies. In a lot of ways they're similar to the kinds of different wallets you would fine offline as well, meaning that different wallets that you find will do different functions.

Some wallet programs are designed to be specialized, going for more specialization purposes than anything else, usually focused on security and information holding. These are perfect for someone who only want to focus on one cryptocurrency at a time, and to make sure that what they earn is safeguarded against people who would want to get their information and hack into their accounts to steal their money. While a lot of their security measures are pretty standard, a lot of times these sort of specialized wallets offer services offline as well such as customer service numbers you could call, IP tracking, printable forms, and such like that.

On the other end of the spectrum though you have wallets that are designed to be more universal. Often these wallets will have a myriad of different options for holding different kinds of cryptocurrencies, not just Ethereum coins. These are usually used for people who are more broad in their investments and are especially useful for those that do eventually want to invest in more than Ethereum. A lot of universal wallets have room inside for all the different cryptocurrencies in place, even for ones designed as a joke. One of the best things about these types of wallets is that you can even use them to transact with other people who use a similar program, exchanging one type of cryptocoin for another. It's not uncommon to see people trading less valuable coins for Ethereum or other high valued coins.

For the purpose of starting out, however, it's often safe to just start with the wallet program that comes with Ethereum on their website. Not only is this wallet highly specialized and focused on the Ethereum coin itself, but it's also tied in with the company that developed the altcoin so you'll have no problem troubleshooting if any problems arise. It's highly recommended that if you do seek out other wallet programs out there afterward, though, to do your research beforehand so that way you don't end up scammed, and having your hard earned investment taken from you.

With that said though the next thing you have to focus on is your internet access, and securing your computer from outside intrusion. This goes without saying, though, as it's often a smart idea to provide protection for your computer, even if you're not involved in the Ethereum trading business, but by reminding yourself to keep yourself protected you'll run less of a chance in the future of having your coins stolen from you. Simple firewall extensions, rootkit tools, anti-virus, and even anti-malware tools will help ensure that no one has access to your information via backdoor programs. Always make sure to backup any valuable information, including wallet information, pool information, or even business information and be vigilant.

Chapter 5 - The Pros and Cons of Ethereum Trading

So now you've gotten an idea of what you want to do when it comes to Ethereum Coin trading, or at least, that's the hope. You've decided how you want to earn them, and how you want to invest and store them, and probably more than likely taken stock of your computer, resources, wealth, and maybe even downloaded a wallet as well to take a look at. That's the idea that's being assumed at the least if you've made it this far in the e-book guide.

But now, you're completely unsure about why you'd want to even invest in the first. So far in this guide, you've seen a small bit of history on cryptocurrency development, delved into the legality of the digital currency, and even learned about Ethereum Coins, what they can do, and how you can earn them, but little on why you should even bother to do so. After all, if their legality comes into question, if they're so hard to earn through mining methods, and only a small number of different Internet vendors are dealing with them, then what's the point? Why not just forgo it altogether and invest your money in something more standard like an index fund, bonds, or anything?

All of those are actually quite valid questions, and the truth of the matter is that investing in cryptocurrencies such as Ethereum, and other altcoins themselves is risky. It's a new form of investment that's only been recent and hasn't even been established for a decade yet. Any cryptocurrency; Ethereum, Bitcoin, Litecoin, or any of the others are highly volatile and are not protected by any form of insurance. If their value plummets, you're out. However, Ethereum by and large due to its wide range of options is actually safer than most other coins when it comes to being used as an investment, and this chapter is going to focus on both the Pro's, and the Cons of the Ethereum market so that way you can be an informed investor who knows the risks when it comes to investment.

Pro's

- One of the most stable coins there is. It was only touched on a little bit when it was mentioned about the volatile nature of cryptocurrency investment, but out of all the different altcoins that are on the market, Ethereum is actually one of the most stable altcoins that you can invest in. Unlike Bitcoin, the most well know altcoin out there, Ethereum hasn't seen massive downward trends in its value. It'll dip occasionally but hasn't seen a drop below 30% of its value since its inception, and is projected within a few years to overtake Bitcoin on the market. This mostly is helped by the stability of the coin, and the nature of the platform itself. As all people who own Ethereum are considered a part of the organization itself, whether they're investing, trading, or mining. With this shared ownership, it allows people to feel more personally invested in its success as well as its success monetarily.

- The range of options. This was only minorly touched on previously, but the range of options for the Altcoin is almost astounding. With other coins that are there, you simply possess them. That's it. They're a digital possession and nothing more. With Ethereum though you have a way to have more control over them than before. You can create intelligent contracts that are only paid out when certain functions are performed. You can quickly and efficiently create a quick marketplace for trading that isn't reliant on third party applications, or outdated website designs (such as a PHP based website). You can even have payment options where you store them like a bank, and pay out in small increments to another person. You can even break them down further into smaller chunks for easier storage. In fact, you can even trade out Ethereum coins for other coins quite easily. These are just options that are on hand built into the platform without the help of other developers either.

- The rate of returns. It's almost amazing how much the rate of return on the Ethereum coin is. Since the inception of Ethereum, it's seen a rapid rise with little to no major downswing and has seen consistent rates on investment returns roughly around 6% on average. Right now though the market itself is seeing a downward trend in the prices of the coins themselves, but this is mostly due to the way the coins work, as they tend to occasionally "split", so as to allow more coins to flood the market. This isn't unusual, because the more coins that enter the market, the less they're worth initially because people are attempting to earn, trade, or mine for more coins. But generally, the price of a single coin itself returns to a standard price after a while.

Cons

- The number of coins. As was touched on in the last Pro section, the number of coins tend to occasionally double as more coins are introduced into the market. Unlike traditional currency that's either minted or printed as needed, there's only a set amount of altcoins available on the market, which is a major driving force behind the value of the digital currency. The more people want to get involved, the more they'll want the Ethereum coins and are willing to pay for it. What happens then is that after a while, it becomes harder and harder to mine for more Ethereum coins and mining itself slowly "dries" up. What happens afterward, to keep interest in the market, is that the developers then create more blocks to be found and allow the market to be flooded with new, additional Ethereum coins. This split momentary drops the price of the coin as their scarcity has now practically doubled in numbers, allowing for miners to find more coins. The entire economic value of the coins in total might be the same, but the individual price of each coin drops. This means that you can buy a single coin for $10, and eventually see it "split" and lose part of its value, dropping to around $8 before it ultimately does return to its original price. This isn't necessarily a bad thing, but if you time your investments wrong it'll be a while before you can recoup your losses. It's generally accepted that the best time to buy an Ethereum coin is right after the market opens up for additional coins to be mined.

-The volatility of returns. As was stated in an earlier section of this guide, the volatile nature of investments means it's entirely possible that you could lose out majorly if you don't understand market trends. It's not uncommon for other investors of cryptocurrencies to invest a certain amount of capital into the altcoins, only to see the market on that altcoin suddenly bottom out, losing a massive amount of money in the process. Generally, those are performed with "pump and dump" coins designed to garner attention and then be sold once traditional currencies are involved. Ethereum, for the most part, is stable and separate from traditional currency, so it won't likely bottom out. However, it's still possible that you won't see substantial returns in any true amount of time depending on how you time the market.

Overall, though, the above points for both the Pros and Cons are only designed to be a matter of opinion based on the market trend of the Ethereum platform. Ultimately the choice is left up to you as someone who wishes to engage in Ethereum trading on how much you want to be involved.

Chapter 6 - Final Thoughts

Investing is always risky. Even in so-called "safe" bets, there is always the chance that you will lose some of your money in investments. This isn't a bad thing, as this is a part of what it is about investments that make them so good to be a part of. You're essentially risking part of your wealth for a bigger reward in the end. It all depends on how much you're willing to risk.

However, with that said some words of caution should be said. Ethereum Trading and Investments are great, but should never be a sole form of investment. Most investors who specialize in being able to move money around and make a living from it will use the age old adage "never put all of your eggs in one basket."

What this means is that only a portion of your money should go into investments in any cryptocurrencies. Ethereum or otherwise. It's often speculated that because the Cryptocurrency market is so young, it'll see a boom within another decade or two once the kinks from the system will be worked out. However, caution is still advised because of the age of the market, and growing too big too quickly could see disastrous effects. So it's usually advised that only about 20% of any excess savings should go towards Cryptocurrencies, and even then only in usual safe bets, which Ethereum is a part of. For every $100 put into any investment, only $20 of it at a time should ever be put into cryptocurrencies.

Still, with all of that said that shouldn't scare anyone off. For every horror story of someone who invested fully in a cryptocurrency, Ethereum included, there are three positive stories to take it's place of people who bought in early, saw a sharp rise in their rate of return, and made some really good money. These sort of people are the people who this book is targeted towards Individuals who didn't know about it at first, but who were interested and who decided to gather information on the market and see how it worked. They're the sort of people who believe fully in the Ethereum platform and what it can do for commerce, and who not only hold coins as a way of investing for the future but also who sell their services. They're also the sort of people who know how money works and aren't just wanting to throw their money at the cryptocurrency market and expect something back.

This entire guide is assuming that you as an individual are intelligent enough to not buy into any hype, and are capable of making sound financial decisions on your own. Everything within this ebook is presented as factual information found throughout the internet from various other investors in Ethereum and internet marketers, all condensed into an easy to understand 6 Chapter guide.

While everything is still up to you in the end, if you do decide to get into the Cryptocurrency Market, and give Ethereum a try, good luck! It's a fun, thrilling ride, and being a part of a fast-growing market is very exhilarating.

Conclusion

Thank you again for choosing this book!

I hope this book was able to help you to gain a better understanding of Ethereum and cryptocurrencies in general. Hopefully you now have an understanding of how you should go about trading and investing this promising new cryptocurrency.

The next step is to get started with Ethereum as it has incredible potential!

Finally, if you enjoyed this book, then I'd like to ask you for a favor, would you be kind enough to leave a review for this book? It would be greatly appreciated! Please feel free to give your honest opinions as this could help me make improvements.

Thank you and good luck!

www.ingramcontent.com/pod-product-compliance
Lightning Source LLC
Chambersburg PA
CBHW070228210526
45169CB00023B/1380